The Reisläufer: The History and Legacy of the Famous Swiss Mercenaries from the Middle Ages to the Modern Era

By Charles River Editors

A depiction of Swiss mercenaries crossing the Alps

About the Author

Sean McLachlan is a historian and archaeologist who has explored ancient sites throughout Europe and the Middle East. He has written numerous books and articles on history and is also the author of several works of fiction, including the *Masked Man of Cairo* series of historical mystery novels and the Civil War horror novel, *A Fine Likeness*. Learn more about his work on his Amazon page and Facebook page.

About Charles River Editors

Charles River Editors is a boutique digital publishing company, specializing in bringing history back to life with educational and engaging books on a wide range of topics. Keep up to date with our new and free offerings with this 5 second sign up on our weekly mailing list, and visit Our Kindle Author Page to see other recently published Kindle titles.

We make these books for you and always want to know our readers' opinions, so we encourage you to leave reviews and look forward to publishing new and exciting titles each week.

Introduction

Hans Holbein the Younger's *Bad War*

When historians are asked to pick a point in history when Western Civilization was transformed and guided down the path to modernity, most of them point to the Renaissance. Indeed, the period revolutionized art, philosophy, religion, sciences and math, with individuals like Galileo, Leonardo, Michelangelo, Raphael, Dante, and Petrarch bridging the past and modern society. The Renaissance also spawned the use of the label "Renaissance Man" to describe a person who is extremely talented in multiple fields, most notably Leonardo da Vinci, who found time to be a painter, sculptor, architect, musician, scientist, mathematician, engineer, inventor, anatomist, geologist, cartographer, botanist, and writer.

However, while the Renaissance is remembered mostly for art and advances in philosophy and thinking, it's often overlooked that the era was also a transitional period in the history of warfare. The Middle Ages have long been remembered for armored knights battling on horseback and armies of men trying to breach the walls of formidable castles, but what is generally forgotten is that medieval warfare was constantly adapting to the times as leaders adopted new techniques and technology, and common infantry became increasingly important throughout the period. Meanwhile, political and technological progress led to continuous change of tactics and equipment. Cavalry became ascendant, only to be later replaced by infantry as their weapons improved, and by the end of the period, warfare was radically changing thanks to the rise of gunpowder weapons such as the handgonne and the bombard.

Artillery and handgonnes had been known since the early 14th century but only became effective near the end of the 15th century, when they were the final factor in the infantry revolution and began to change warfare forever. By the middle of the 15th century, artillery was knocking down castle walls that had stood for generations. Infantry also proved their worth with powerful longbows and tight formations of polearms upsetting the long dominance of mounted, heavily armored knights, and handheld firearms threatened to make armor obsolete. New types of warriors were developed, and new tactics had to take the emerging era of black powder weapons into account, ushering in a time of great change in military strategy, tactics, and technology.

The Middle Ages witnessed almost constant warfare in Europe, so mercenaries were a constant on the battlefield, but the 15th century also saw the rise of mercenary usage by the increasingly wealthy aristocracy. At the time, England and France existed in smaller versions than in the modern age, while the Spanish had unified into a few large kingdoms and were slowly pushing the Moors off the Iberian Peninsula. Norway and Hungary were larger than they are now, but otherwise, most of Europe was a patchwork quilt of small, constantly warring states. This was especially true in Germany and Italy, where innumerable city-states and little fiefdoms struggled to gain more territory and defend themselves against their neighbors.

Switzerland, ringed by the Alps, was divided into numerous small statelets called cantons, with some in the valleys and some further up in the mountains. There was a great deal of local infighting like elsewhere in Europe, but by the Late Middle Ages, unification seemed possible for a few reasons. Most notably, the Swiss felt threatened by larger outside states such as the Holy Roman Empire, France, and Milan, which were poised to take advantage of Swiss division and relative weakness to invade. The Holy Roman Empire was an especially great threat because it had some political claim over the Swiss cantons, although the Swiss had always enjoyed a great deal of independence from Hapsburg rule. Furthermore, some important trade routes ran through the region, and all the cantons would benefit if these routes were kept open and secure.

In 1291, three cantons around Lake Lucerne—Schwyz, Uri, and Unterwalden—formed the so-called "Everlasting League" to counter outside aggression. This became the nucleus of what would develop into the Swiss Confederacy, and eventually the nation of Switzerland. Gradually, more and more cantons would join, ending their constant, low-level infighting and making the land more secure for trade. By the beginning of the 16th century, the Swiss Confederacy was comprised of 13 cantons, and this voluntary unification, without threats or conquest, was remarkable for the time. It was helped by the fact that the Swiss had a roughly similar culture, and that the region, with its ring of protective mountains, made the advantages of unification against a hostile outer world obvious to all.

Few powers dared try to enter Swiss territory, and they

generally met with disaster when they did, but ironically, this led to a new problem. The Swiss villages had always been prone to fighting and raiding one another, maintaining a constant low-level warfare that made the Swiss good fighters, and hotheaded young men wanted a chance to fight. At the same time, other areas, especially Italy, saw a growing need for mercenaries. Constantly trying to take land from their neighbors, Italian city-states were hampered by the fact that most of their men were busy tilling fields, engaging in trade and crafts, or building the cities and monuments that would become the wonders of the Renaissance. Moreover, the cutthroat politics of the city-states were such that rulers could not trust their own officers, who might murder them and take over their positions, something that happened on numerous occasions.

The obvious solution was to hire mercenary armies, units of foreign men who had no connections or loyalty to any of the local factions and who would fight for money. The Swiss were perfectly poised to fill this need, given that they were geographically close and many already spoke Italian. They were also well trained thanks to a well-organized system of local and canton militias. With mercenary units being organized on the canton level, it was often possible to hire an entire, ready-made army with a single contract, and not only did these armies come already armed and trained, but they came from the same local area. They could all speak the same language, unlike the hodgepodge of mercenaries hired by some noblemen, and because they came from the same geographic area, indeed were often neighbors from the same village, they had a sense of personal loyalty to one another. This was vital in any battle, where a soldier had to be able to rely on the man he was standing beside.

In short order, other nations like France and Hungary sent emissaries to the cantons to hire soldiers as well, and the legend of the Swiss mercenaries, some of the most famous fighters for hire in the history of warfare, was born. *The Reisläufer: The History and Legacy of the Famous Swiss Mercenaries from the Middle Ages to the Modern Era* examines the events that led to the rise of the mercenaries, what their lives and battles were like, and their impact. Along with pictures depicting important people, places, and events, you will learn about the Reisläufer like never before.

Medieval Warfare

In the 14th century, medieval warfare started to change from being dominated by cavalry to giving a larger role, and eventually a dominant role, to the infantry. Several weapons were key to what historians often call the "infantry revolution," including longbows, crossbows, pikes, handgonnes, and polearms.

A polearm is a staff weapon that has a head that can perform more than one function, such as cutting, chopping, impaling, or pulling an enemy off his horse. One of the most common and longest-lived type of polearm is the halberd, which can chop and impale. It made its first appearance at the Battle of Morgarten on November 15, 1315. Austrian knights advanced through a Swiss pass and were ambushed by Swiss fighters using halberds, attacking from the rocks above. The knights were slaughtered and the halberd became a standard Swiss weapon for centuries. It's still carried today by the Pope's Swiss Guard.

David Ball's picture of reenactors with halberds

Polearms proved effective in many battles and were a

mainstay of the armies during the Wars of the Roses. Using a simple polearm adapted from a branch cutter, they could unhorse knights and cleave through armor. Like the Swiss halberdiers, they fought in formation. Unlike pikemen, however, a single man bearing a polearm was still dangerous, while pikemen needed large numbers and a tight formation to be effective.

Pikes were iron-headed spears with shafts measuring from 14 to 18 feet. Seasoned ash was the favored wood as it was strong and flexible. This heavy, awkward weapon required a great deal of training to be used properly. Entire military manuals were dedicated to a complex set of drills for using pikes in formation, although in battle, there were generally only a few movements used. The Swiss were so well-trained that pike squares of up to 10,000 men could maneuver across the battlefield with ease.

For holding the line against a cavalry charge, the men in the front rank would crouch with the butt of the pike resting against the right instep while holding the pike at an angle that put the point level with the horse's breast. This stance was called "charge for horse." The second rank, and sometimes a couple more ranks behind them, held their pikes in the "charged" position, with one hand gripping the butt-end of the pike while the other gripped the shaft.

For fighting against fellow infantry, the front three to five ranks held their pikes level in the "charged" position. The rear ranks held their pikes at an angle above their comrades' heads in the front ranks. If a man fell, the file of men of which he was a part moved forward a rank so the space would be filled.

Pike formations were first developed by the Swiss in the 15th century, loosely based on similar formations in ancient Greece. Just as the Greeks strengthened their hoplite pike formations with archers and slingers on the flanks, the Swiss had highly-trained crossbowmen and handgonners firing at the enemy in an attempt to break their formation and keep enemy archers and handgonners at bay.

Another important weapon in the infantry revolution was the crossbow. The crossbow harkens back to Roman times, when large examples called *ballistae* were used in sieges and to send large bolts cutting through enemy formations. Handheld crossbows existed too as a hunting weapon. Smaller handheld crossbows reappeared in medieval Europe in the 11th century as a military weapon, especially among the Normans and Spanish. While they were more powerful and easier to use than the bows at the time (the longbow had yet to make its appearance) they did not replace bows because they were all but impossible to aim beyond about 80 yards. The trouble was that any bolt or arrow flies in an arc due to the pull of gravity, so firing at anything beyond that range required tilting the crossbow upwards so much it obscured the view of the target.

Another weapon vital to the infantry revolution was the longbow, which has already been mentioned in several of the battles already discussed. While the bow was used throughout ancient times and the Middle Ages, on mainland Europe it was mostly replaced by the crossbow in the early 13th century. This would change with the introduction of the longbow, a more powerful weapon than the traditional hunting bows. The original longbowmen were Welshmen recruited by King Edward I of England after he conquered Wales.

The weapon got its name from the fact that it was almost as tall as the man using it. This gave it a longer draw and therefore more force. Longbows were generally made of yew, a strong and pliable wood. The longbow was cheap and easy to make, but required extensive training to be used well.

In the 14th century, the old feudal levies began to be replaced with methodical enlistment for regular pay. Feudal levies were always unreliable for long campaigns since there was a natural desire to return home to take care of the fields. Short forays into enemy territory could be profitable, but no one wanted to miss planting or harvest. Soldiers being paid a regular wage were more likely to stay, and in the 15th century standing armies began to become the norm.

The main purpose of most campaigns was booty. The land would be ravaged, stripped of its valuables, its buildings burned, and its fields laid to waste. This weakened the enemy at planting time and made it more difficult for them to launch their own campaign. Commanders often avoided an open battle as these could be risky. If too many of the nobility got killed, it would seriously weaken the kingdom and cause internal strife. Leaders would try to fool the enemy as to their intentions, and if a battle seemed unavoidable, try to catch the enemy by surprise.

The nobility would not be riding their best horses on the march. Instead they would ride ordinary horses in order to keep their best warhorses rested for any battle. Likewise, neither they nor the regular troops would wear armor unless contact with the enemy seemed imminent.

Armies would march and fight in three main divisions—the vanguard, the main guard, and the rearguard. The vanguard would be in front, the main guard or *bataille* in the center, while the rearguard took up the rear and protected the wagon train. These three main units stayed the same even in battle, having set places on the line.

While pitched battles have always caught the imagination of the chroniclers, artists, and modern historians, they were in fact quite rare until about 1300. In fact, they were generally fought only as a last resort to stop an invasion. Battles were risky affairs, where important members of one's ruling class could be killed or permanently disabled. At Bannockburn in 1314, the English nobility lost somewhere between 154 and 700 of its members. At Crécy, more than 1,200 knights lost their lives, including nine princes. More than 15,000 other ranks also died, but that was less important in the minds of the nobility. Almost as bad, and far more common since battles often had a low mortality rate, were the nobles lost to capture, for they would subsequently be ransomed for exorbitant amounts.

Sieges were a better way to capture territory. The pioneering work of military historian Jim Bradbury specified the "six S's of siege warfare:" suborning or subverting key defenders, scaring the garrisons with propaganda, sapping the walls, starving the population, storming the defenses, and shelling the defenders. Cities, not castles, were the main focus of siege warfare because cities offered wealth and a taxable population. Castles were often set at key geographic points so that invading armies would have to invest them.

A siege required preparations on both sides. Many siege engines included complex parts that had to be made beforehand and brought with the invading army. Foragers would spread out across the countryside to secure as much food as possible for the inevitable waiting game with the defenders.

For their part, defenders would strip the surrounding countryside of all food, fuel, and forage in order to shorten the time the attackers could stay in the region. They would also send out sallies to harass the attackers and destroy important siege engines and artillery.

As with the infantry and cavalry, there was an arms race between armies and castle builders. Castles at the beginning of our period were simple affairs, generally wooden stockades with a ditch. The Normans were masters at this sort of fortification in the 11th century. Their motte-and-bailey castles consisted of an area enclosed by a wooden stockade, plus an artificial hill also enclosed by its own stockade and holding up a wooden tower. The whole fortification would be surrounded by a ditch. Motte-and-bailey castles were quick and cheap to construct and were widely used after the battle of Hastings in 1066 to secure the English countryside. The Anglo-Saxons, having no siege engines, found it difficult to take them.

As time went on, many of the wooden towers and walls of the more important motte-and-bailey castles were replaced with stone. Stone castles developed elsewhere in Europe too. At first they were simple square keeps with surrounding walls and a wet or dry moat to add another level of protection. Towers were set on the corners, pushing out from the line of the walls to allow archers crossfire against anyone trying to storm the walls. Arrow slits were set at regular intervals in the towers and walls and the walls themselves were topped with crenellations, a jagged series of stones that allowed the defenders to hide while reloading their bows.

Various other siege engines were used to bombard enemy fortifications. The simplest was the catapult. These were wooden arms on frames that would be pulled back using torsion to build up potential energy. The end of the beam had a shallow bowl that held a stone or bundle of flaming pitch. When the torsion was released, the beam would snap up and be stopped at 90 degrees by a crossbeam. The missile would then fly forward. A number of these could batter at the walls or throw stones into the city beyond. Incendiary devices could start a fire inside that would demoralize the defenders and hasten their surrender. Fire was always a danger in crowded medieval cities, but attackers would think twice about burning down a city they wanted to make their own.

A more powerful stone thrower was the trebuchet, which was a large beam with a heavy counterweight. The beam would be pulled down and let go, and the counterweight would make the end of the beam fly up. A sling on the end of the beam would then release a stone. Trebuchets were often quite large and the chronicles say that the largest could throw stones weighing up to 350 pounds. A modern reconstruction at Warwick Castle in England weighs 22 tons, stands 59 feet tall, and can throw an 80 pound stone up to 980 feet.

Luc Viatour's picture of a trebuchet

Gunpowder

Gunpowder was invented in China in the 8th or 9th century AD, and its use slowly spread through South Asia and the Middle East before making it to Europe in the late 13th century. The famous scholar Francis Bacon gave a recipe for it in a book written in 1267, but for a time it was a mere curiosity. The first record of a cannon in Europe comes from a manuscript written in 1326, which has an illustration showing an armored man with what looks like a slow match lighting a vase-shaped object. An arrow is shooting out of the opening. This crude cannon was called a *pot de fer* in French and *vasi* in Italian. A small specimen weighing 20 pounds has survived in Sweden and is 12 inches long with a 1.5 inch bore. Records show they fired large iron or wooden quarrels with metal fins halfway along the shaft. The rear of the shaft would have been padded to better contain the expanding gases of the exploding powder.

Eventually, medieval engineers developed a new type of cannon in the form of a large cylinder made up of iron bars fused together and strengthened with hoops like a barrel. In fact, this is where the term for the "barrel" of a gun comes from. These devices were called *cannons* or *bombards*. The arrow was replaced with a sphere of stone or lead, both materials being cheap and easy to work. These cannon balls proved to be more aerodynamic and generated more impact than the old-style arrows.

Cannons were quickly brought into use both for sieges and pitched battles. The earliest reference to cannons being used in sieges was the siege of Friuli in Italy in 1331, but it's unclear when they were first used in the field. They may have been used at the battle of Crécy in 1346. It is certain that both the English and French armies were equipped with cannons, but none of the eyewitness accounts of the battle mention them, only a few later histories written decades later.

Bombards grew in size, with some reaching epic proportions. For these giant cannons, the balls would be made of stone because using so much lead would have been prohibitively expensive. This increase in size was encouraged by the development of cheaper gunpowder. Until the late 14th century, saltpeter, a key ingredient in gunpowder, had to be imported from India or found in the rare natural conditions that encouraged its formation. By the end of the 14th century, Europeans had figured out how to make their own saltpeter and production increased to industrial levels.

Large bombards proved effective at knocking down castle walls. The first recorded instance of this was at the siege of Saint-Sauveur-le-Vicomte in 1375, and cases are frequent thereafter. It is interesting to note that the siege of Saint-Sauveur-le-Vicomte used 200 pounds of gunpowder, an impossibly lavish supply before prices for gunpowder dropped. Soon supplies of gunpowder for sieges and campaigns would be measured in the thousands of pounds.

While thick walls, curved towers, and sallies by the defenders to destroy the besieging artillery kept early artillery from being a game changer for quite some time, as soon as the walls of Saint-Sauveur-le-Vicomte crumbled, the days of castles and walled cities were numbered. Even so, reducing a fortified position remained a major undertaking. The 1466 siege of Dinant in Belgium took a week and 1,700 shots. Sometimes attackers ran out of powder or shot, which happened to the Burgundians at their 1475 siege of Cologne.

A picture indicating some of the damage done to Saint-Sauveur-le-Vicomte

It wasn't long after the invention of artillery that gunners began to experiment with smaller, handheld black powder weapons. Cannons had the great disadvantage of being slow and cumbersome. There are several reports of artillery not making it to the battle on time, and even the *ribaudiaux* moved more slowly than the average soldier could march. The solution, of course, was to create a small black powder weapon that could be carried by a single man.

European sources first mentioned the widespread use of handgonnes, as they were often called, in the late 14th century, precisely the time when gunpowder became cheaper. These were short metal barrels stuck on the end of wooden hafts that could be tucked under the arm, the powder being lit through a touchhole with the free hand. While they were not terribly accurate, and had a shorter range and slower rate of fire than longbows or crossbows, they had the advantage of being better able to punch through armor than longbows and crossbows. A second advantage was that they were simple to make and use.

Another type of handgonne was the *hackbut*, or hook gun. These generally had long metal stocks fused directly with the barrel. On the bottom of the barrel was a hook that could be braced against a pavise or wall in order to steady the gun and allow more accurate firing. Since they were designed to be braced, *hackbuts* could be larger than regular handgonnes.

Peasants were using handgonnes right from the start.

When a group of revolting peasants attacked Huntercombe Manor in England in 1375, they carried with them several handgonnes, and handgonnes soon became a common weapon in peasant rebellions and for urban militias. As cities grew in the 14th century, these militias could be quite large. The one of Strasburg is recorded in 1392 as having 20,000 fully armed men ready for action at a moment's notice. Of course, cities would also be centers of gunpowder and handgonne production.

Handgonnes were limited by their small caliber and modest charge of powder. Early gunpowder was not very powerful, another reason that cannons grew steadily larger in size. Around the beginning of the 15th century, however, chemists developed crumbled and corned powder. By wetting the powder slightly and patting it into a cake to be left to dry, the gunpowder could be stored without the ingredients getting separated or absorbing too much moisture. Not only could it be stored longer than early gunpowder, it could then be crumbled into a large-grain powder with higher surface-to-volume ratio that made it burn quicker. This greatly increased the explosive force.

The earliest handgonnes were tucked under the arm and lit manually with a slow match that touched the gunpowder in the priming pan before lighting the main charge in the barrel. Such an awkward firing stance made aiming difficult. Later, a simple lever device held the slow match, called a serpentine. Pressing the level brought the slow match down on the firing pan. This was soon replaced with an actual trigger, and the soldier was able to bring the gun up to his shoulder and look down the barrel, vastly improving the soldier's ability to aim. This gun was called the *arquebus*, and it was the first black powder firearm that looked like a modern rifle. It appeared by the end of the 15th century but was still a cumbersome piece with a barrel measuring three to four-and-a-half feet long with a heavy stock. Arquebusiers used a "rest"—a short pole with a spike that stuck in the earth and a u-shaped rest, similar to an oarlock—to hold the arquebus. As matchlock muskets developed into lighter, more manageable weapons, the forked rest was gradually discarded.

There is some confusion with the terms "arquebus" and "musket," with contemporaries and modern writers sometimes using them interchangeably. The first muskets were actually bigger than the arquebus. By the mid-17th century, however, the term "musket" was generally used for lighter firearms that didn't require rests. By the end of that century, the musket had all but replaced the arquebus, and soldiers carrying firearms were now referred to as musketeers.

The arquebus had an effective range of 50-60 yards. The

ball traveled further, but beyond that distance, hitting was a matter of pure chance. A trained arquebusier could fire every 30-60 seconds. By contrast, the matchlock musket had an effective range of between 100-120 yards, and as it was lighter, it had a slightly faster rate of fire.

To improve the slow rate of fire, arquebusiers wore a bandolier belt with a dozen leather tubes containing measured charges of gunpowder, which the men jokingly referred to as the "Twelve Apostles." A separate bag held the bullets, but in battle, the men often kept the bullets in their mouths to have quicker access to them. The lead turned their lips and teeth green and probably undermined their health.

The matchlock had another disadvantage: the slow match could easily be snuffed out in the rain or even a heavy mist, and a damp slow match couldn't be lit, so it was unreliable in inclement weather. If they expected rain, arquebusiers kept their spare, unlit slow matches under their hats, giving us the expression "keep it under your hat."

Another development was the wheellock, a wound-up, flint-and-steel mechanism that, when the trigger was pulled, spun like a modern lighter, sending sparks into the firing pan. This was no faster to reload than a matchlock, and its complicated mechanism meant that it often misfired. On the other hand, the mechanism made little movement to disrupt aim, and thus was quite accurate for its day.

In pistol and carbine form, wheel locks were also used by cavalry, who didn't have spare hands to manipulate slow matches. Each cavalryman often carried two or more wheel locks, and in the 16th century, a tactic emerged, called the "caracole," in which riders approached slow-moving infantry formations—such as pike squares—in columns. The first rank fired their pistols or carbines and wheel to the left or right to be replaced by the next rank. Thus, a steady, if not particularly accurate, fire could be kept up against the infantry, at least until the riders ran out of shots and had to move away from the fighting to reload their guns. If the enemy was sufficiently broken up by the fire, the cavalry, who were armored and carried swords, could charge at the enemy and try to finish them off. The German Reiters were some of the pioneers of this tactic, starting in the 1540s.

Students of military history will recognize the caracole maneuver as an updated version of methods used by horse archers, such as the Parthians and Mongols. Ancient accounts of battles were avidly read by Renaissance military theorists and leaders, and the lessons learned centuries before were reintroduced with updated technology.

It would not be until the full adoption of the matchlock and further improvements in gunpowder that full plate armor would disappear. Armor was still useful against other weapons, and until the full development of the matchlock, handgonnes remained inaccurate, short-range devices. They tended to be used in conjunction with other weapons, with handgonners most commonly being teamed up with crossbowmen. Crossbows were more accurate and had a faster rate of fire, and although crossbow bolts were less likely to punch through armor, they could provide a good covering fire, harassing and slowly diminishing the enemy until they got close enough for the handgonners to deliver a deadly volley.

Handgonnes, even in their simple form, spread quickly throughout Europe. Many castle owners modified the arrow slits on their walls, cutting circular holes in them to accommodate handgonnes or small cannons. By the late 15th century, handgonners had become a major part of the leading armies. An account about the army from Milan in 1482 mentions 1,250 handgonners, 233 crossbowmen, and 352 arquebusiers. The arquebus was expensive to make, so for a time the more primitive handgonnes remained in use for the bulk of the men, but crossbows were clearly on their way out.

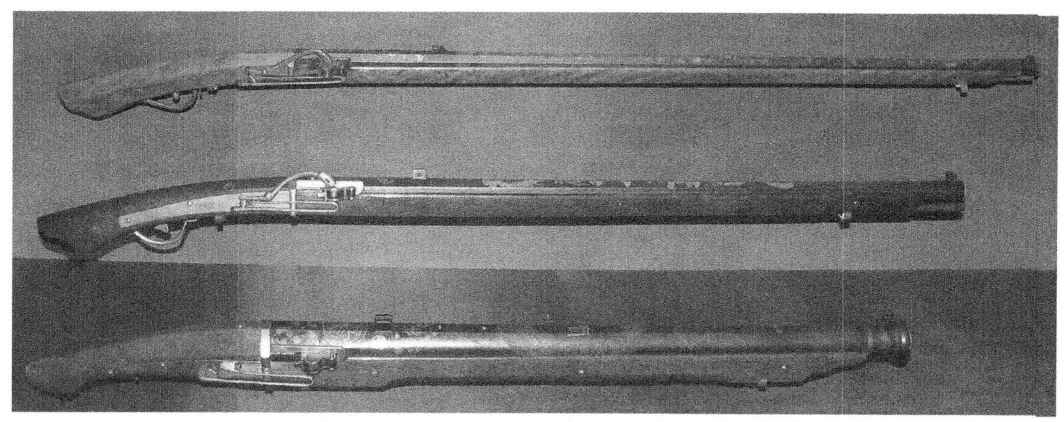

A picture of Italian arquebuses

The most effective early use of handgonnes and artillery was by the Hussites in their rebellion against the Holy Roman Empire from 1419-1436. This was an army composed mostly of peasants and civilians from small towns in the Czech homeland, strengthened by the retinues of a few rebellious nobles. They were fighting for their independence against an advanced and experienced army.

Knowing they couldn't defeat the Holy Roman Empire in a simple fight on the open field, the Hussites used their rural resources and skills to the utmost advantage. Their principal innovation was the *wagenburg*, a moving wall of fortified farm wagons with wooden planks fastened to their sides fitted with firing holes. Archers, crossbowmen, and handgonners could fire from them in relative safety. Some wagons were equipped with cannons. The wagons could be chained together and drawn into a circle to make a fortress that could be easily disassembled and moved elsewhere.

Each wagon was equipped with tools in order to dig entrenchments and was manned by two drivers, two handgonners, six crossbowmen, fourteen men with flails, four men with halberds, and two men carrying pavises. The pavisiers would block off the spaces between wagons and give the crossbowmen and handgonners not in the wagons themselves a space from behind which to shoot.

As can be seen, much of the equipment was readily available in any peasant village—flails, digging tools, and carts. Handgonnes and halberds were easy enough for the village blacksmith to make. Crossbows and gunpowder required specialized labor to make but little training to use.

The Hussites used their wagenburgs in a tactic of offensive defense. They would wheel the mobile fortress near an important road or town, circle the wagons, and wait. The enemy, faced with having the Hussites near some key point, would have no choice but to attack. Fighting from behind fortified wagons, the Hussites negated most of the advantage enjoyed by mounted knights. This tactic worked so well that other armies began to adopt it. Within a couple of generations, however, more mobile and powerful artillery made the wagenburgs vulnerable and they were discarded.

Charles the Bold

Charles the Bold

Arguably the most advanced army before the start of the 16th century was that of Charles the Bold, Duke of Burgundy, who ruled from 1467-1477. He tried to unify his fragmented kingdom by buying up the best soldiers he could, including mounted forces, English longbowmen, Italian Condottieri as armored cavalry and infantry crossbowmen, handgonners, and pikemen. The army was highly organized and blended different types of soldiers to take advantage of their best aspects while compensating for each other's weaknesses. His pike formations were mixed with archers and handgonners to provide covering fire and drive away enemies shooting at the formation. Likewise, mounted longbowmen rode with the heavy armored cavalry to provide covering fire from the flanks.

The most advanced wing of Charles the Bold's army was the artillery train. The falcon cannon looked much more like a modern artillery piece than the earlier bombards. Mounted on a wheeled wooden frame with an adjustable barrel, it offered much more maneuverability and accuracy than any competing artillery.

By the 1470s, however, Charles the Bold began to meet his match, despite the fact the Burgundian army was the most advanced in Europe. It boasted a large number of feudal lords in full armor, levied a gentry that included many knights and tough mercenaries, all of which were well-organized under a tight command structure. It was a modern army, highly trained with an organized artillery train of the most advanced cannons available. But the Swiss beat the Burgundians at the Battle of Héricourt on November 13, 1474. Burgundian casualties were recorded as 1,617 dead, a large number for what had been a small engagement. Interestingly, the Burgundian force did not have their famous artillery train with them, but both sides had units of handgonners, who fired crude handheld firearms.

The Burgundians suffered defeat again at the much larger Battle of Grandson on March 2, 1476. Both armies numbered about 20,000, and this time the Burgundians had their artillery with them, but they only fired a few shots because the Swiss pikemen advanced remarkably rapidly to engage the Burgundian infantry and cavalry. The Burgundians were unable to get through the line of pikes, and as their artillery was unable to support them at such close quarters, they soon fled, leaving their camp to be plundered. The Swiss also captured many of their guns, some of which are still on display in Swiss museums.

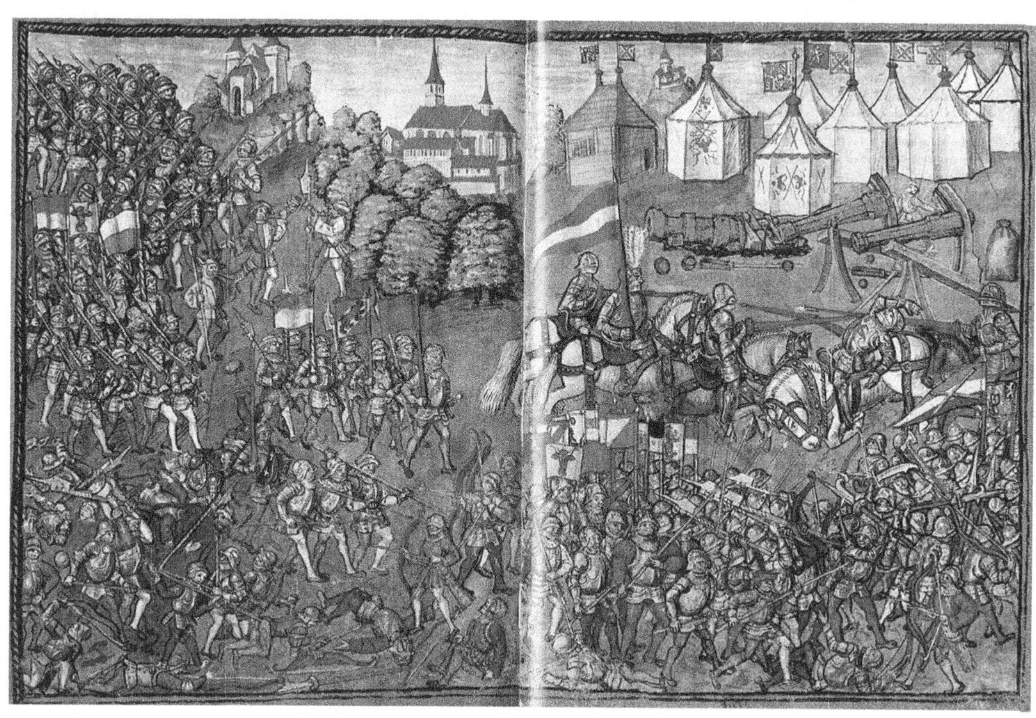

A 16th century illustration of the battle

Charles the Bold's next defeat came on June 22, 1476 at the Battle of Morat. This time, the Swiss outnumbered the Burgundians, but Charles (who was starting to be known as Charles the Rash) engaged anyway. Charles besieged the city of Morat, held by the Swiss Confederacy, and gradually reduced it to rubble with artillery, but when he heard of the approach of a Swiss relief force, he met it in hilly terrain, making the Swiss pike squares less effective. The Swiss marched from this direction and had no choice but to pass through the unfavorable terrain. To further strengthen his position, Charles had his men dig ditches and ramparts, positioning archers and artillery behind them, with one flank being secured by a steep gorge.

The Swiss arrived late, but since it was payday, many Burgundians who were supposed to be guarding the earthworks were back at camp in a disorganized mass, trying to get their money and settle down to eat lunch. The skeleton crew at the earthworks was completely surprised by the unexpected arrival of the Swiss, and though they held on for a time, they were seriously outnumbered and finally broke. The Swiss reformed beyond the earthworks and marched into the Burgundian camp.

The Burgundians tried to rally, but the units were scattered, and they attacked the compact pike square piecemeal and were knocked aside, one by one. Charles had to retreat once again, leaving his camp's equipment behind him.

The final blow came in northeastern France on January 5, 1477. On that day, Charles the Bold led some 8,000 men, although some estimates put his numbers much lower. Facing him were about 12,000 French and 10,000 Swiss.

Once again, Charles besieged a city, this time the city of Nancy, the capital of Lorraine. When the Swiss and French relief force approached, Charles took up position on a heavily wooded slope behind a stream in a narrow valley. He had with him some 30 field guns, but a driving snowstorm reduced visibility to only a few yards, making the guns all but useless.

Despite the poor visibility, the French and Swiss forces had scouted out their position and engaged the Burgundians with a direct assault with a part of their force, while the main force struggled through hilly and wooded terrain to flank the defenders on the left. The force emerged from the woods uphill from the Burgundians and charged down at them.

Charles rallied his men, and they fought bravely but were seriously outnumbered and nearly surrounded. Units melted away as Charles bemoaned the fact that he "struggle[d] against a spider who [was] everywhere at once."

As his formations were broken into smaller and smaller units, Charles found himself isolated with a small number of men, surrounded by attacking Swiss. One Swiss fighter hit Charles on the head with a halberd, breaking through his helmet and killing him. The slaughter was such that it took three days to pick through the bodies to find Charles the Bold, once a feared general but now a symbol of a dying age.

This remarkable series of defeats shows how a well-organized and technologically advanced army could not stand up to innovative infantry tactics. Theoretically, the Burgundian artillery should have been able to blast large holes through the tightly formed pike squares, but they ended up being no match for them. No doubt, the Swiss did suffer losses from artillery fire, but their highly trained pikemen were able to quickly shift location within the square to plug any gaps and advance rapidly enough that the slow-loading cannons could only get off a couple of shots before the pikemen were upon them.

The secret to his enemies' success was the *Reisläufer*, Swiss mercenaries (mostly pikemen) who were poorly disciplined and lacked a strong overall command structure, but were highly trained and motivated in battle. They came from the many independent cantons making up the Helvetic Confederacy in what would become Switzerland, and though Switzerland is now a centralized nation, at the time it was a place of constant low-level fighting between cantons and neighboring villages. The young men were well-accustomed to brawling, and each village was drilled with the pike and other weapons to stand against more serious attacks.

This was the key to the Swiss' strength. Not only were they highly trained in the use of the pike, halberd, short sword, and dagger, but they were also fiercely loyal to the men beside them, who were their friends, neighbors, and relatives. This created a far more cohesive unit than a bunch of people drawn up by feudal levy and led by some noble to whom the men had never spoken. The Swiss, on the other hand, were led by the *schultheiss*, a local noble with a much closer relationship to the men than his lowland counterparts. Sometimes, the schultheiss wasn't nobility at all, but some local hero who had risen to prominence through ability and charisma.

The First Swiss Mercenaries

As weapons technology and infantry tactics changed, the Swiss Confederacy was one of the most innovative forces in Europe. Warfare had always been a common man's pursuit in the Swiss lands, as groups of commoners would fight their neighbors or occasionally unite with them if foreigners tried to march over the Alps. As a result, the Swiss were efficient at summoning large numbers of trained men in a short period of time, something other regions had difficulty managing. Records show that by the middle of the 15th century, when the Confederacy consisted of eight cantons, they could use conscription to summon 54,000 men, a vast army by the standards of the time.

This conscription was organized by councils of elders at the canton and local levels. Able-bodied men were divided into three categories - the *Auszug*, the *Landwehr*, and the *Landsturm*. The *Auszug* were the best of the lot, consisting of young, unmarried men between the ages of 18 and 30. Older men willing to go on campaign made up the *Landwehr*. Everyone else was in the *Landsturm* and were only called up in times of crisis, usually to stave off an invasion. Each city, guild, and local area kept detailed records of how many men they could offer to the war effort and what types of weapons they would carry.

The local governments saw to it that each man was trained in the arms they were expected to carry, as well as in basics such as marching, understanding orders and signals, and the other knowledge necessary to make a good soldier. In this they were far beyond most regions of the time, who relied on knights, a few trained troops, and a mass of untrained and undisciplined men of little use on the field. In the Swiss armies it was the common man, not the elite, who was trained in fighting. The Swiss mentality was that infantry, not cavalry, should be the main fighting force in battle.

Any man called to serve had to bring several days' worth of food with him, thus easing the quartermaster's job. Interestingly, on many campaigns this would be enough for the army to get out of the cantons. Once in foreign territory, it was considered fair game to live off the land, and one didn't have to rob one's neighbors.

Command was organized on the canton and local level, with supreme command of the army in the hands of the *Feldhauptmann*, chosen either by the canton council of elders or by representatives of all the army units by popular vote. His staff consisted of various officers and orderlies, and even an executioner called a *Weibel*, a much-feared man with the power of life and death over the troops.

The main standard of the army was carried by an ensign called the *Venner,* who bore personal responsibility for the banner, looked at by the troops as an almost sacred object. Indeed, many banners have survived to this day in Swiss museums, a testament to the care they were given. Since the *Venner* had the typical duties of a second in command, in battle he had another man actually carry the banner, which would be guarded by heavily armed elite bodyguards.

There were many other banners in the Swiss army besides the main one. Each canton, guild, city, town, and village would have its own, serving both as a rallying point for that particular unit and as a point of pride. The flags of the larger units would be accompanied by drummers, fifers, and bagpipers, and they came in an incredible variety of designs and styles that reflected the unit's history and background. At the beginning of a campaign, the men would swear by their flag and by the supreme flag to do their duty and follow the regulations of war set down by the commander.

Indeed, the flags were so important that the standard unit of a Swiss army was called the *Fähnlein* ("small flag") and numbered 50-150 soldiers. The unit flag would have two men exclusively to carry and guard it. The *Fähnlein* could be further subdivided into a 10-man *Rotte*.

On the march and in battle, the army was divided into the *Vorhut* in the vanguard, the *Gewalthut* in the middle, and the *Nachhut* in the rear. These were organized by an officer called the *Ordnungsmacher*. Each unit would be given an exact position on the march and in deployment, a level of organization far more detailed than most armies of the day. Inevitably, the relative sizes of the *Vorhut*, the *Gewalthut* and the *Nachhut* could be changed depending on the circumstances, such as the army having to divide or because of the situation they faced on the battlefield.

The Swiss became one of the prime mercenary groups in the 14th century. Of course, such a profitable business was quick to attract men of other nations, so the Swiss had competition from the very start. Among them were the *Condottieri*, Italian mercenaries who were known for making detailed contracts with their employers that outlined the rights and responsibilities of both sides. Starting in the late 15th century, the Swiss and the *Condottieri* had to compete with the *Landsknechts*, German mercenaries who mostly fought for the Holy Roman Empire. From further afield came Spanish and Balkan mercenaries, and even Ottoman Turks. If men were willing to fight and abide by their terms of service at least most of the time, they could find work.

Of course, with so much money on the table, rivalries were bitter, and when the Swiss and the Landsknechts found themselves facing off, no quarter would be expected or given.

Swiss Armor

Swiss soldiers were expected to purchase their own weapons and body protection, so an army would have a wide variety of armor types. The weapons, of necessity, were more standardized. Often guilds paid for arms and armor for their members, ensuring they stood out as better units, something of a point of pride for them. Guilds even marched under their own unique banners. Anything lost or damaged in service was replaced or repaired by the canton.

At the start of the 14th century, only the nobility would have full suits of plate armor. Most men, if they were lucky, might have a metal breastplate or a suit of chainmail, as well as a steel helmet. A cheaper alternative, because it was simpler to make, was the "coat of plates." These was made up of overlapping plates riveted together and attached to a leather undercoat to protect the torso. Since it was several pieces and not one, it wasn't as strong as a proper suit of plate armor, but it did provide a fair degree of protection. Other cheap armor options included a leather shirt or quilted, padded shirt with metal studs or plates sewn onto them. This provided some protection, but not nearly as much as the knights and nobility enjoyed.

Many men also wore suits of hardened leather. Leather armor was much lighter and cooler than metal armor, though not as resistant to blows. Many Swiss mercenaries wore a combination of chainmail and leather backing with a layer of quilted padding. Leather armor was generally *cuir bouilli* ("boiled leather"). Leather would be placed in boiling water, which made it elastic and pliable, and it was then hammered into shape as it shrank, thickened, and hardened. Each piece could be hammered into its proper shape much like metal to create a full suit of armor.

Experiments with modern reenactors have demonstrated that wearing metal armor in cold weather saps the heat out of the body, even when the person is exerting himself, and it has the the reverse effect in hot weather. Thus, men tried not to wear their armor except when they knew they were on the verge of a battle.

The Swiss generally did not carry shields. The halberd and pike were both two-handed weapons, and the men who stood between the ranks with heavy axes and two-handed swords also could not carry shields. Conversely, crossbowmen, handgonners, and arquebusiers often hid behind an oversized shield called a pavise. This device was named after the Italian city-state of Pavia, where they originated in the 13th century. These convex shields made of wood or hardened leather were big enough for a man to completely cover himself while reloading and were kept upright by a spike or a prop secured into the ground. Those used by handgonners and arquebusiers often had a space cut out at the top to poke the barrel through while the man remained covered except for the top half of his head. The pavise was rather unwieldy, so it was generally used in defense where the men had prepared a position, or in the static fighting of siege warfare.

Accompanying the army were drummers and horn blowers. The drummers were used to keep time on the march and for other signals. This was typical of many armies throughout history. The Swiss also favored musicians with horns, especially a large war horn called a *Harsthörner*. This curved horn, as big as a man's arm, let out a powerful blast and must have echoed wonderfully in the Alpine valleys of their homeland. Its sound initiated the advance and could be heard over the din of battle. Several of them blowing at once were used to intimidate the enemy.

The Swiss in Battle

The Swiss first started flexing their military muscle against the outside world at the Battle of Morgarten on November 15, 1315. A little over 20 years before, the cantons of Schwyz, Uri, and Unterwalden had created their "Everlasting League" in order to show their independence from the Hapsburg rulers of the Holy Roman Empire, and now that independence was put to the test.

In 1315, Schwyz had sacked the monastery of Einsiedeln, which was under Hapsburg protection, in an open act of defiance. Unable to stand this insult, the Holy Roman Empire sent a force of 9,000 men to attack the cantons, including about 2,000 heavy cavalry. This army was led by Leopold I, Duke of Austria, who moved quickly to cut off the canton from outside help, so only a few reinforcements from Schwyz's two allied canons managed to get through. On the day of battle, the Swiss could only field 1,300 men.

The terrain was hilly and rough, and the ground was made even more impassable by a complex network of palisades and earthworks that made cavalry maneuvers impossible. The only practical way forward was through the pass at Morgarten, so Leopold ordered his men through the pass, with his cavalry in front. As the path narrowed, they found the road blocked, although a thin track on the left, hugging a steep wooded slope, remained clear and passable. To the right the slope ran down to the shores of Lake Ägeri.

At this point Leopold should have smelled a trap, but nevertheless, he led his men along this track, thinning out his line and lengthening his column to half a mile long in order to fit. When they got to the hamlet of Schafstetten, they met their first real resistance, a small force of Swiss who put up a stout defense. This brought the vanguard to a halt, but thanks to poor communications the rest of the column continued to move forward, bunching up just behind the fight and making the path more and more crowded.

It was at this point that the Swiss pounced. Appearing out of the woods came the bulk of their force, the slope giving their charge an additional momentum. They rolled boulders and logs down at the packed Austrians, knocking many off their horses and panicking the mounts. Then they swept down and smashed into the chaotic, milling line with axes and halberds.

The foot soldiers at the back of the column hurried to escape, but many stumbled into some marshes and got cut down by their pursuers, while the knights at the vanguard fared even worse. Totally cut off and with all order gone, it was each man for himself as the Imperial troops desperately tried to cut their way free. Some managed to gallop back down the road, trampling their own infantry in the process.

The Austrians lost about 2,000 men that day, while Swiss casualties were said to only be a dozen. While this lopsided result may be the product of a bit of exaggerating on the Swiss side (the Austrians certainly didn’t stick around to count enemy casualties), there is no doubt that Morgarten was a crushing defeat for the Hapsburg knights. The three cantons renewed their treaty of alliance and other cantons began to join, the first being Lucerne in 1332.

The Hapsburg defeat did not end their claims over the Swiss cantons or their valuable trade routes through the Alps. Several battles followed in the ensuing years, out of which the Swiss usually emerged the victors. Time and again the simple foot soldier armed with a halberd proved himself capable of defeating a heavily armored knight, at least when the knights were kept from charging *en masse*.

One key battle came in 1386, by which time the Swiss Confederacy had expanded to eight cantons. Duke Leopold III, a member of the Hapsburg dynasty who ruled over the western portions of the empire, wanted to reassert his family's claims on the cantons. He used the hostilities between Lucerne and the Hapsburg fortress of Rothenburg, and the canton's signing of pacts with several border towns and valleys under Austrian control, as an excuse to declare war. There had been many skirmishes between the cantons and Hapsburg border strongholds as the cantons tried to expand their sphere of influence.

A 16th century portrait of Leopold III

As Leopold set about organizing his army, he tried some psychological warfare on the Swiss by sending declarations of war from various noblemen who controlled towns or territories near the cantons. A total of 167 did so, and to strike fear in Swiss hearts, the messages were sent in groups over the period of several days. Thus, just as the Swiss were reading declarations of war from a dozen or so nobles, another messenger would appear with 20 more. Ultimately, this did not have the intended effect, and the Swiss prepared to fight.

Despite his ambitions and plenty of time to prepare, Leopold III could only field about 4,000 men, a mixture of around 1,500 knights and the rest mercenaries from Italy, Germany, and France. He moved into Swiss territory, looting one town and reaping the Swiss harvest as he went, before coming upon a force of 1,600 Swiss. They met at the hamlet of Hildisrieden, near Sempach, on July 9.

It seems surprising that the Swiss could not muster more men considering their lands were being invaded. This was likely because they initially thought Zurich would be the target and the men from that canton rushed to that city to defend it. Also, a slow response from other cantons kept any greater force from being mustered.

The terrain was rough, with the smaller Swiss force taking up position on some wooded high ground. Leopold III, remembering how this had put Hapsburg knights at a disadvantage in previous engagements, ordered his heavy cavalry to dismount. He formed them up in a tight line holding their lances forward like pikes. This, he hoped, would offset the feared Swiss pike.

The Swiss formed a wedge, an effective method for piercing a line. Unfortunately for them, Leopold III's tactic turned out to be effective and in a grinding melee, his knights began to inflict heavy casualties on the poorly armored Swiss. Some of the Swiss had no more armor than a wooden plank tied to their left arm as a crude sort of shield.

One would think that greater numbers and far better armor would decide the battle, but another factor came into play: the weather. It was a hot summer day, and the Hapsburg knights, encased in full armor and having to slog up a hill to fight, were soon sweltering. Their movements became slow and uncertain, while the Swiss continued to fight in better condition. It would have been better for the Austrians to send the lighter armored mercenaries into the fray, but the knights worried that the mercenaries would finish the Swiss off and steal their glory.

As the battle ground on, both sides suffering in different ways, the Swiss sent their left rear of the wedge around the Hapsburg flank. This, and the timely arrival of Swiss reinforcements, helped turn the tide.

Often in battles where forces with long weapons are pushing against one another, a small break in one side's line will lead to collapse. This is, according to legend, what happened at Sempach. A Swiss soldier named Arnold von Winkelried threw himself on the knights' lances, breaking several and lodging others in his own body. This gave the men immediately around him a chance to strike down the now unarmed knights, form a breach in the Hapsburg line, and get a foothold in the Hapsburg position. From there they smashed their heavy halberd blades down on the heads of the Austrian knights, their fellows pushing them back with their points. The gap grew until the line broke.

Like many such stories, it is uncertain if it's actually true. The first mention of Arnold von Winkelried's heroism is in the Lucerne Chronicle of 1513, long after the battle.

Seeing his front buckle, Leopold III urged his second line to attack, but they did not keep formation over the rough ground and the Swiss, finally breaking through the front line, charged at them and broke the second line too. The rearguard fled, taking most of the horses with them. The stranded knights of the front and second lines were soon slaughtered. By the end of the day, an estimated 1,800 Imperial soldiers lay dead alongside only 200 Swiss. Among the Hapsburg losses were some 400 noblemen, including Duke Leopold III himself and the flower of the Hapsburg nobility.

A fresco depicting the battle

This decisive and rather surprising victory helped strengthen ties among the young Swiss Confederacy, which up until this point had been a rather loose collection of otherwise very independent cantons. It also allowed for Swiss expansion into the border areas that had been the root cause of the hostilities. The Swiss rightly view the Battle of Sempach as one of the key moments in the establishment of their nation. A chapel was built at the site to thank God for the victory and a restored and expanded chapel stands there to this day. The battle also firmly established the halberd as the primary weapon of the Swiss.

It was not to remain so. While it served well in several subsequent battles, such as at Näfels (April 9, 1388), where the Confederacy again defeated a much larger Hapsburg force, within a generation a new weapon was being introduced: the pike. The Battle of Arbedo on June 30, 1422 is generally considered by military historians as the watershed moment when the halberd stopped being the main weapon of the Swiss Confederacy. This time the enemy was the Duchy of Milan, which would be a rival of the Confederacy throughout much of this period as the two sides struggled over control of lucrative trade Alpine routes to France.

In this case the fight was over the city of Bellinzona, which the Swiss bought from the local barons. The Milanese offered to buy it in turn, but the Swiss rejected this, leading to the Italians taking it by force. Subsequently, the Swiss moved in to threaten the city, and the Milanese sent an army of 16,000 men, including about 5,000 cavalry, led by the Italian *condottiero* (mercenary captain) Francesco Bussone da Carmagnola. Once again the Swiss could muster far fewer forces, only being able to field 2,500 infantry (some sources say 4,000), mostly armed with halberds. They had emerged victorious from such long odds before, and hoped to do so again.

After failing to take the city, the Swiss returned to their camp, unaware that the Milanese relief force was close. The Milanese launched a surprise attack.

One would think given the element of surprise and overwhelming numbers, that the Milanese would have made short work of the Swiss, but the Swiss rallied quickly and formed into a tight square with their halberds. The Milanese cavalry launched attack after attack on them, only to be repulsed with heavy losses. The Milanese cavalry then dismounted and rearmed themselves with pikes. Many of the Italian infantry also had pikes and the longer weapons began to take a toll on the Swiss ranks, who began to give ground. Milanese crossbowmen firing from the flanks also helped wear down Swiss resistance.

At this point, the battle was all but won, but Francesco Bussone didn't do his men any favors by loudly declaring that no quarter would be given, as this only strengthened the Swiss resolve. That and the timely arrival of 600 Swiss foragers, who the Milanese thought were the vanguard of a larger relief force, saved the Swiss army from annihilation. The Milanese fell back to reform, and the Swiss used the opportunity to hack through a thin screening force and escape.

The Swiss lost about 500 dead and 300 captured, a third of their force. The Milanese lost about 1,000 but won the battle, and Bellinzona would not become part of the Swiss Confederacy until 1500.

The obvious superiority of the Milanese pikes over the

shorter Swiss halberds made the Confederacy reconsider its tactics. It ordered that all cantons to increase the proportion of pikes to halberds in their formations, and the Confederacy further ordered that men be trained in their use and on how to march and fight in pike formation.

It is important to note here that while the Swiss were the most famous pikemen of the late Middle Ages and early Renaissance, they were not the first troops in that period to use the weapon. Indeed, the rough terrain of their homeland did not encourage the development of tight pike squares, but as Swiss troops were increasingly employed beyond the Alps, often as mercenaries, the more open terrain encouraged the use of the weapon. It wasn't long before Swiss pikemen, and the tactics they employed, became the most advanced in all of Europe.

The first test of the new system came just two years later, at the Battle of St. Jakob an der Birs, on August 26, 1444. The Hundred Years War had ended just three months before, and the French King Charles VII had a large army of French mercenaries called the Armagnacs with nothing to do. Worried these rough men might start causing trouble in France, he decided to have them cause trouble elsewhere, so Charles allied with the Hapsburgs to form an army of 40,000 men, mostly Armagnacs, to invade the Swiss Confederacy.

The huge army pushed into Swiss territory with little trouble until they came upon a force of 1,500 Swiss, more than a quarter of whom were armed with 18-foot pikes. Despite being vastly outnumbered and being told to wait for reinforcements, the Swiss couldn't control themselves and decided to stand their ground and fight the French and Hapsburgs. They formed into three pike squares, with those armed with halberds or other weapons taking up the centers of the squares.

The Swiss then did something even more remarkable: they advanced. One would figure given their numerical inferiority that they would hold their ground and allow the enemy to grind themselves down on the pike wall, but instead they decided to push the enemy off the field of battle. This would not be the last time the Swiss charged with their pikes.

Initially, the Armagnac cavalry held their ground, backed up by weight of numbers, and the battle became a grueling and bloody stalemate for five hours. After this time, the Swiss were utterly spent and could not bring in fresh troops, while the Armagnacs could cycle in new men whenever they wanted. The Swiss withdrew in good order to the hospital of St. Jacob, which was surrounded by a wall.

This turned out to be a mistake. Now that they were

holed up inside, the Armagnacs brought in archers to fire arrows at a high angle to fall behind the wall while artillery blasted holes in it. The Swiss died in droves, and before long, the walls were a heap of rubble. The Armagnac infantry moved in to finish them off, and the Swiss army died to a man. Ultimately, their defeat was not in vain, because the invaders had lost so many men that they called off the invasion.

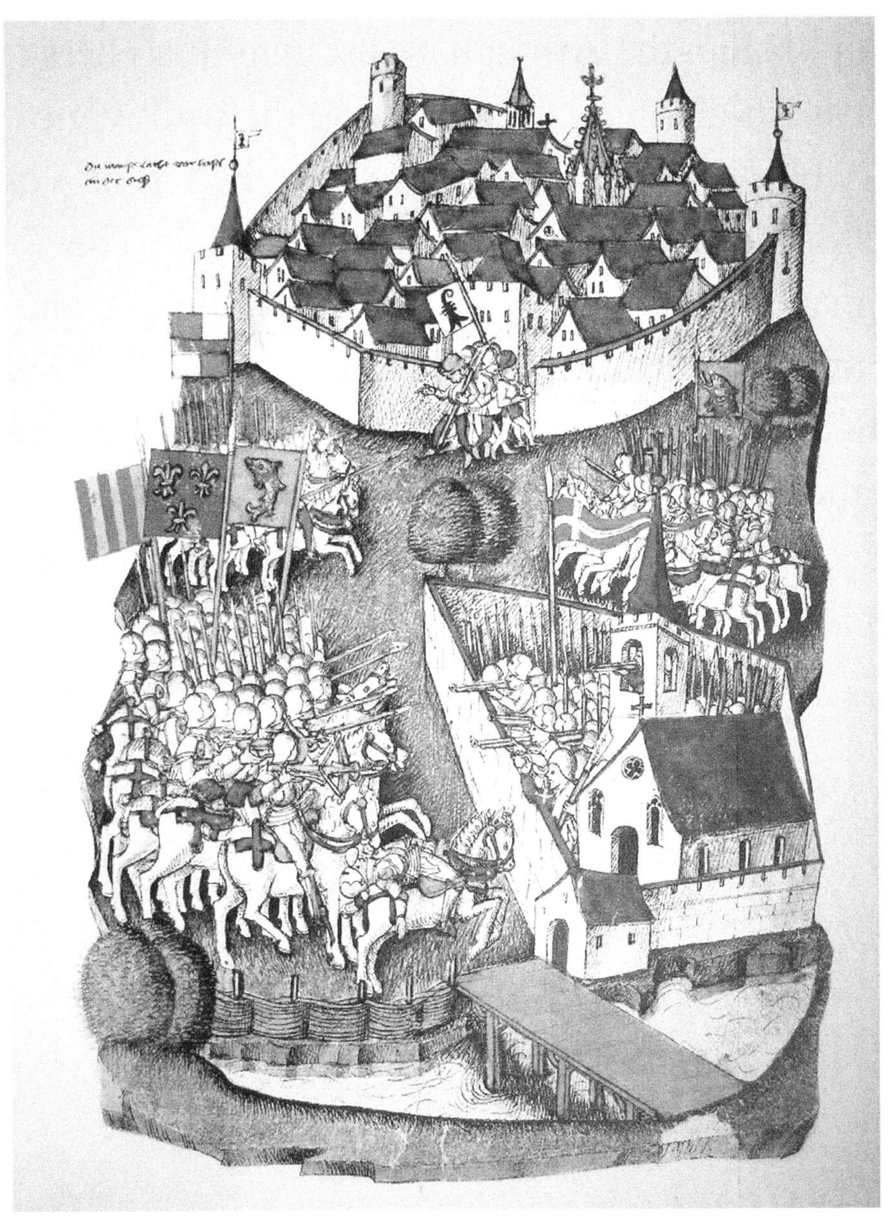

An illustration of the battle

While the Swiss suffered defeat at the Battle of St. Jacob-en-Birs, the heavy casualties they inflicted, nearly 4,000 men, proved the worth of the new weapon, and it would be adopted in greater proportional numbers in the following years. It would also signal to the Swiss that they needed to invest in artillery, crossbows, and handgonnes.

This they did, and it helped balance out their main weapon, which would remain the pike until well into the 16th century.

One big test of Swiss mettle came during the Burgundian Wars of 1474-1477. Charles the Bold, Duke of Burgundy, had trained a modern and elite army and decided to go on a campaign of expansion against most of his neighbors. The Burgundian army was a mix of old and new, including a large number of feudal lords in full armor, levied gentry that included many knights, and many tough mercenaries, all well organized under a tight command structure. One major innovation was a highly trained and organized artillery train of the most advanced cannons available.

The first time this army came up against the Swiss was at the Battle of Héricourt on November 13, 1474. The Burgundians had advanced too quickly to have their artillery with them, although they did have a large number of handgonners. The Burgundians lost, taking heavy casualties. The Swiss pikemen had fared well, especially since they had a sizeable number of handgonners themselves to fight back against the Burgundian ranged weapons. If it was not for them, the Swiss might have been taken down bit by bit by the crude yet deadly black powder weapons. Pike squares need to be supported by a good ratio of crossbowmen or handgonners to avoid this.

The Swiss did not always remember this important truth.

The Swiss defeated the Burgundians again at the much larger Battle of Grandson on March 2, 1476. Both armies numbered about 20,000, and this time the Burgundians had their artillery with them. It only got to fire a few shots, however, because the Swiss pikemen charged into the teeth of the fire to close with the Burgundian infantry and cavalry. The Swiss had enough sense to know that they couldn't stay still when facing such advanced and accurate artillery, and the men had enough courage to go forwards instead of backwards. This strong charge soon broke the Burgundian line and the Swiss set about plundering their camp. They also captured the enemy artillery train, which they put to good use in later engagements. Some of the Burgundian cannons are still on display in Swiss museums.

A depiction of the battle

The Swiss defeated Charles the Bold again on June 22, 1476 at the Battle of Morat. The final blow came in northeastern France on January 5, 1477 at the Battle of Nancy, where Charles was fighting against the Duchy of Lorraine. On that day, Charles led nearly 8,000 men, although some estimates put his numbers much lower. Facing him were about 12,000 French and a force of 10,000 Swiss mercenaries.

Charles was besieging the city of Nancy, capital of Lorraine, when the Swiss and French relief force approached. Charles took up position on a heavily wooded slope behind a stream in a narrow valley. He hoped this strong position would hamper any Swiss pike charge and he had with him about 30 field guns ready to blast the enemy lines apart. A driving snowstorm reduced visibility to only a few yards, making these guns all but useless. Despite the poor visibility, the French and Swiss force had scouted out the position and decided to engage the Burgundians with a direct assault with part of their army to keep them occupied while the main force struggled through hilly and wooded terrain to flank the defenders on the left. This group emerged from the woods uphill from the Burgundians and charged down at them.

While Charles rallied his men and they fought bravely, they were seriously outnumbered and nearly surrounded. Units began to melt away as Charles bemoaned, "I struggle against a spider who is everywhere at once."

As his formations got broken up into smaller and smaller units, Charles found himself isolated with a small number of men, surrounded by attacking Swiss. One Swiss fighter hit him on the head with a halberd, breaking through Charles's helmet and killing him. The slaughter was such that it took three days to pick through the bodies to find that of Charles the Bold.

The Swiss mercenary continued to be used by many European powers throughout the late 15th century and well into the 16th century. One important battle was fought at Novara on June 6, 1513. This time the Swiss were fighting for the Duchy of Milan as mercenaries against the king of France, who wanted to take the duchy as it was the only way to expand further into Italian lands. The Swiss, naturally, preferred to have several small city-states on their doorstep rather than a powerful kingdom, so they readily hired themselves out to their old enemies the Milanese. The Swiss had helped place Massimiliano Sforza on the throne as the Duke of Milan at the end of 1512, so the duke was friendly toward the Swiss Confederacy, something the king of France most certainly was not.

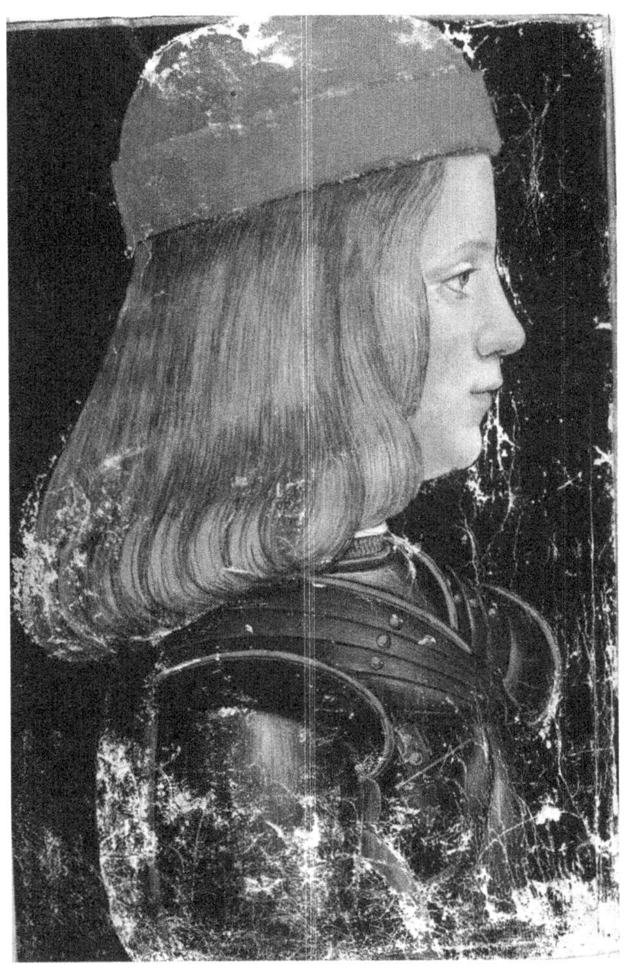

Sforza

In 1513, the French marched over the Alps, no small feat with heavily armored men and lumbering artillery, and moved into the Duchy of Milan to besiege the city of Novara and its garrison of Swiss mercenaries. A Swiss force, in a series of forced marches, rushed to relieve the city before it fell.

The two sides met on June 6, 1513, and this time the French and their Landsknecht mercenaries faced the forces of Milan and their Swiss Confederate mercenaries.

The French fielded an army of 1,200 heavy cavalry, 600 light cavalry, 14,000 infantry, 6,000 Landsknechts, 2,500 bowmen, and 28 cannons. They faced a force of mostly Swiss pikemen. While the historical sources vary as to their numbers, ranging from 11,000 to 20,000, they all agree that it was an inferior force both in numbers and in branches of service, lacking significant cavalry and artillery.

The Swiss advanced quickly, managing a deft maneuver to come at the French from multiple directions. The French artillery did deadly work against the packed troops, taking down an estimated 700 men in just three minutes, but then the Swiss closed, and the tide of battle shifted. At first the Landsknecht pike squares held against the Swiss, but the Swiss encircled the French camp, hemming in the French cavalry so it couldn't deploy properly, and captured the French guns. Beset on all sides, the French and German units broke one by one.

A general slaughter ensued as the Swiss descended on their hated rivals the Landsknechts, and the Swiss showed no mercy even as hundreds of Landsknechts surrendered. The French force lost around 7,000 men and the Swiss at least 1,500.

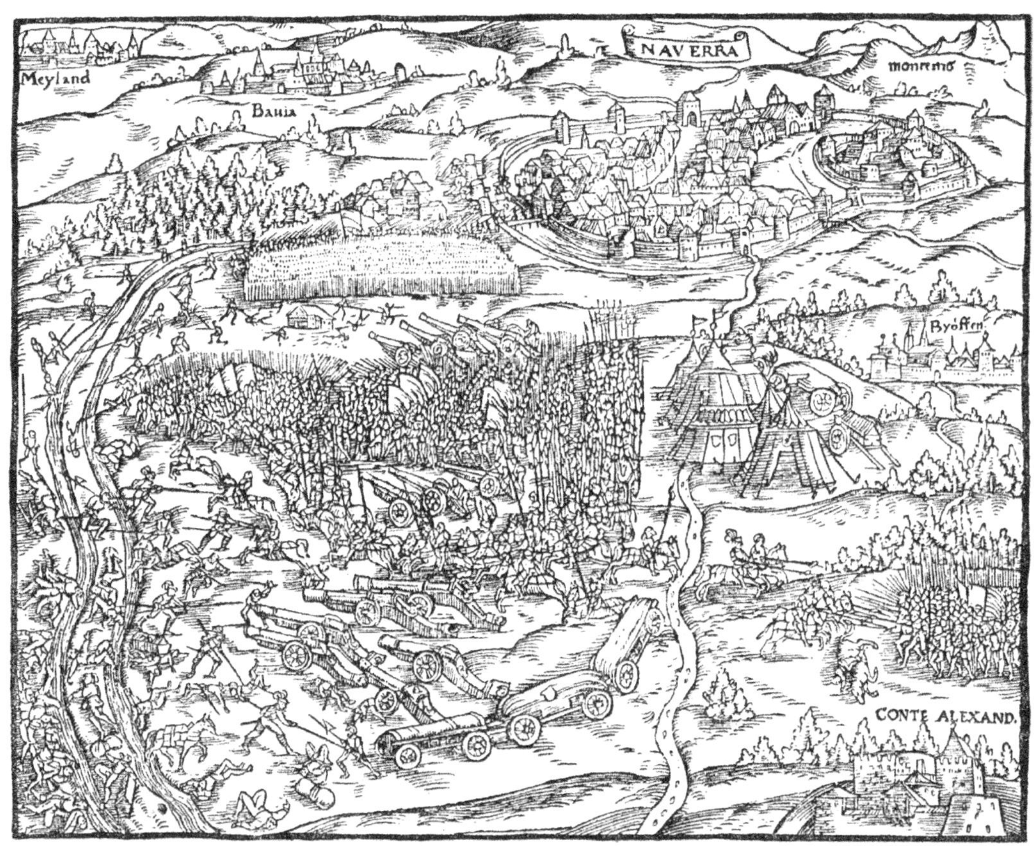

A 16th century woodcut engraving of the battle

The French headed north in full retreat. The Swiss, not having any cavalry to pursue, were not able to properly harry them, but they did follow them all the way to Dijon. The French king eventually paid them to leave France.

The French returned two years later and only just managed to defeat the Swiss mercenaries at the Battle of Marignano on September 13-14, 1515 in a brutal slugfest. After both sides suffered heavy losses, the French gained Milan and the Swiss signed a peace treaty with France that forever gave up their interests in Italy. This and the divisions created by religious debates between Catholics and Protestants back in Switzerland meant that the Swiss would play less and less of a role in European warfare and politics in the years to come.

Of course, even if the Swiss Confederacy as an entity played less of a role in European politics, that did not mean Swiss mercenaries were out of the picture. They had several more battles to fight, one of the most significant being the Battle of Bicocca on April 27, 1522. This battle is interesting for having involved all the major mercenary groups of the day, including the Swiss, the Landsknechts, and the Condottieri. It is also significant in that the affair was mostly resolved with firearms and artillery.

The engagement was one of the most significant of the Italian Wars of 1521-1526. Once again, foreign powers were struggling over control of northern Italy. The war saw Francis I of France and the Republic of Venice fighting against the Holy Roman Emperor Charles V, Henry VIII of England, and the Papal States. A large number of Swiss mercenaries entered French service and played a significant part in the fighting.

A combined French and Venetian force commanded by Odet of Foix, Viscount of Lautrec, faced off against a combined force of troops from the Holy Roman Empire, Spain, Milan, and the Papal States led by Prospero Colonna, an Italian condottiero. Both sides used large numbers of mercenaries. The bulk of the Viscount of Lautrec's infantry was Swiss pikemen, along with some Italian Condottieri of the famous elite Black Bands. Prospero Colonna also brought along Condottieri as well as Landsknechts.

Colonna

In the opening move of the war in late 1521, the French were ejected from Milan but stayed close to the city to try and cut the enemy's lines of communication and force them to withdraw. Colonna kept his own side moving constantly, not engaging with the French and hoping to wear them down and force them to leave.

In the end, Colonna's strategy worked after a fashion. This war of maneuver was cut short by the Swiss, who, complaining that they had not been paid, insisted on closing with the enemy in a decisive battle that would bring a swift end to the campaign. Many had already deserted, and the rest threatened to unless there was a battle soon. Faced with losing the bulk of his infantry, Lautrec had no choice but to go against his better judgment and force the enemy into an engagement. His position was strengthened by the arrival of 16,000 more Swiss mercenaries, newly hired and ready to fight. They were joined by fresh French troops and the newly hired Black Bands led by the condottiero Giovanni de' Medici. He now had somewhere between 19,000 and 31,000 men (sources vary). It was now or never.

In response to threatening moves by Lautrec, Colonna moved out of Milan with at least 18,000 men and into the manor park of Bicocca, about four miles north of the city. Lautrec didn't want to attack an army of roughly equal size in an entrenched position, but once again the Swiss forced his hand - the new arrivals hadn't been paid and threatened to leave if Lautrec didn't attack. Ever impulsive, the Swiss preferred to risk all in order to win a swift victory and the chance of booty, rather than a dreary, indecisive campaign with no payment in sight.

For his part, Colonna had picked an excellent defensive

position. The French would be coming from the north, but the manor park of Bicocca was unapproachable to a large body of men and artillery from the west thanks to a wide area of marshy ground. The eastern boundary of the manor park was delineated by a north-south road leading to Milan. Running to the west of this road was a deep, wet ditch. The only easy crossing point was a stone bridge some distance to the south of the manor park. To come at this bridge, the French would have to move along the road, exposing their flank, and then cross a relatively narrow and easily defended bridge. Lautrec was unlikely to try this, but Colonna protected the bridge with some cavalry and 6,400 infantry under the condottiero Francesco Sforza just in case.

The obvious line of attack was from the north, across a broad field cut by irrigation ditches, the southern edge of which was cut by a sunken road running east to west. This front measured only 600 yards wide, allowing Colonna to densely pack his defending forces behind the sunken road. To further strengthen the position, Colonna had his men deepen the road and use the excavated soil to make a rampart along the southern edge of it. He even built artillery emplacements jutting out from the earthwork so artillery could be swung to the left and right and get a good field of fire, much like the artillery turrets in the "star forts" that were being developed in Italy at this time.

Guarding this formidable position were four ranks of Spanish arquebusiers backed by Spanish pikemen and German Landsknechts, as well as a number of cannons.

Despite Colonna's strong position, the Swiss insisted on attacking. First the Black Bands moved through the field to force out the Spanish pickets, which had been put there to slow any advance and harass an attacking force. Clearing them out would help the advance go more smoothly, and the advance would need all the help it could get.

After that, Lautrec ordered forward his Swiss pikemen, two large blocks of 4,000-7,000 men each (sources vary), and with them came the artillery. The rest of the army was arrayed in two broad lines to the rear. The plan was to set up the guns and bombard the defensive position while the Swiss waited out of range. Once the Imperial guns were taken out and the position softened up, the Swiss would move in.

As it turned out, the Swiss refused to wait for such prudent tactics. The two columns had a rivalry going. One was made up of men from rural cantons, while the other consisted of men from Bern and other cities. They taunted each other, asserting that they didn't have the guts to charge. In the end, both of them did before the artillery had a chance to fire a shot.

The Imperial artillery, on the other hand, enjoyed wonderful shooting. With the Swiss struggling in densely packed formations across a rough and open field, they couldn't have asked for a better target. Cannonballs and shrapnel ripped through the Swiss lines, and yet the Swiss forged ahead. Historians estimate they lost a thousand men before they even reached the earthworks.

That was where they stopped. The road had been cut deep enough and the earthwork was piled high enough that their 18-foot pikes couldn't reach the arquebusiers on top. The Spaniards fired volley after volley into the crowd of Swiss, inflicting terrible losses. A few brave pikemen managed to clamber up through the teeth of the fire to gain a position on top of the ramparts, only to be pushed back down by the Landsknechts.

After half an hour, the Swiss gave up and retreated, leaving 3,000 dead on the field and sunken road. Many of the Imperial troops were eager to follow up this crushing move by charging the French lines, but Colonna forbade this. The rest of Lautrec's army was fresh and intact, his artillery was set up, and Colonna didn't want to turn a victory into a defeat. Even so, some Spanish troops, too eager to be controlled, rushed out after the Swiss, only to be pushed back by the Black Bands.

Meanwhile, the French sent 400 cavalry along the north-south road to Milan and reached the bridge behind the Imperial position. They fought their way across the bridge and into the Imperial camp, but Colonna sent some cavalry reinforcements and was able to push the French cavalry back across the bridge. The cavalry retreated to the main French lines.

With that, the battle was over. The French forces had lost more than 3,000 men, mostly Swiss mercenaries killed in that one bloody charge. While the Imperial losses have not been recorded, they were quite small. The Swiss returned to their cantons and the French army, considerably weakened by their departure, soon quit northern Italy.

This battle had a lingering effect on Swiss morale. As the contemporary Italian statesman Francesco Guicciardini noted, "They went back to their mountains diminished in numbers, but much more diminished in audacity; for it is certain that the losses which they suffered at Bicocca so affected them that in the coming years they no longer displayed their wonted vigor."

This proved quite correct. No longer were the Swiss willing to launch the hellbent charges that had made them both feared and famous.

As that battle proved, the well-trained and steady Spanish arquebusiers decided the day, and their black powder infantry weapon was really coming into its own thanks to advances in technology and tactics. Instead of laboriously putting in the correct measure of powder, followed by wadding and shot, arquebusiers now carried a dozen premeasured packets containing the correct amount of powder and a musket ball. The gunmen humorously dubbed these "the twelve apostles." To load, the arquebusier would tear off the top of the packet with his teeth and pour the powder into the muzzle. Then he would ram the wrapper and ball down the muzzle with a ramrod. A bit more powder poured into the firing pan from a powder horn, and the gun was ready to fire. This greatly increased the rate of fire over the old-style handgonnes.

It's important to note that the Spanish had four ranks of arquebusiers. Once the first had fired, it was trained to pull back and let the next rank aim and fire while the first rank reloaded. Then the second rank would draw back to give room to the one behind and start reloading. Thus, a nearly continuous fire was possible. The only problem with this was that black powder weapons give off a great deal of smoke. With hundreds of arquebuses belching out clouds of white, gritty smoke over the course of hours, the entire battlefield would get shrouded in "the fog of war." This seriously hampered aiming at anything further than point blank range, but it also hampered the enemy's firing as well. There are many cases in the pike and shot era of both sides calling an unspoken truce to let the smoke clear before resuming hostilities. Smokeless powder wouldn't be developed until the end of the 19th century.

The crushing defeat at Bicocca did not end French designs on northern Italy, and they would return in October of 1523 with an army of 18,000 men commanded by Guillaume Gouffier, Lord of Bonnivet. They were soon joined by an equal number of Swiss mercenaries. Prospero Colonna was still in the region, but his numbers had been reduced to 9,000 men and he had no choice but withdraw to Milan.

This could have been a great opportunity to retake Milan, but Bonnivet thought Colonna had far more men than he actually did and thus withdrew a bit from the city and set up winter quarters. Colonna sent for help, and by the time the spring campaigning season started, he had 15,000 Landsknechts and a large number of Spanish troops.

The two sides finally clashed at the Battle of the Sesia River on April 30, 1524. As at the Battle of Bicocca, the Spanish arquebusiers decided the day, delivering withering fire against the unsupported Swiss pike squares and making many of them abandon the French army. This time, the Imperial army chased the French over the Alps all the way to Provence, taking the provincial capital of

Aix-en-Provence on August 9 and besieging the important port of Marseilles. They were not able to take it before French reinforcements forced them out of the region, but they left the countryside ravaged.

In October, the French King Francis I himself led an army across the Alps, numbering nearly 40,000 men, in a final bid to take northern Italy. The troops spread out to take as much territory as possible, and Francis led 26,600 men, including 8,000 Swiss mercenaries, to besiege the city of Pavia. They clashed with a 22,300-strong Imperial relief force on February 24, 1525. The Battle of Pavia would be one of the most influential battles of the century, but the Swiss didn't have much of a role. They were badly treated by the Landsknechts, and another 3,000 Swiss who had been manning the siege lines were overrun when the garrison in Pavia made a sortie.

As his divided and defeated army fled, King Francis found himself isolated with only a small number of members of the Black Bands and some Swiss. They were eventually surrounded and vastly outnumbered by Imperial troops. Francis ended up a prisoner and was forced to sign the humiliating Treaty of Madrid, in which Francis, among other concessions, renounced all claims in Italy, Flanders, and Artois. He also was compelled to surrender Burgundy and agree to send two of his sons to live as hostages at the Spanish court.

The poor showing of the Swiss pikemen in the Italian Wars of 1521-1526 sullied their reputation and sapped their morale. They had suffered too many defeats, shown themselves too vulnerable to gunfire, and had left their posts too many times. The glory days were over.

The Modern Era

With increasing competition and the rise of larger nations, the demand for Swiss mercenaries waned. Their golden age had passed, and Switzerland retreated into its now familiar role of heavily armed neutrality.

Some Swiss still hired themselves out as mercenaries, however. Their efficient and effective pike square remained in demand throughout the 16th century, although after the lesson learned at the Battle of the Sesia, commanders made sure to back them up with a sufficient number of firearms. This style of warfare, known as "pike and shot," was the main style of fighting until the end of the 17th century.

One battle that stood out in this period was the Battle of Dreux (December 19, 1562), fought during the French Wars of Religion (1562-1598). The battle, which was the opening round of the war, saw a unit of Swiss pikemen marching with the Catholic forces under Anne de Montmorency against a Huguenot army led by Louis I, Prince of Condé. The Huguenot force was marching into

Normandy in order to take the region, and the Catholics moved to stop them. The Catholics had 16,500 infantry, 2,500 cavalry, and 22 guns, while the Huguenots fielded 8,500 infantry, 4,500 cavalry, and an unknown but small number of guns.

The Catholics enjoyed superior numbers of artillery and infantry, as well as better quality infantry with many French veterans as well as the Swiss mercenaries. The Huguenot infantry was for the most part poorly trained and armed and with an insufficient number of pikes. They did have a Landsknecht unit to firm up the line, but the Landsknechts were a notable minority. The Huguenots, however, were much superior in cavalry, including many heavily armored French horsemen carrying lances, and they also employed German *Reiters*, armored horsemen who carried wheellock pistols. They had a particular maneuver called the *caracole*, in which rank after rank would fire at the enemy, then wheel to allow the next rank to move up and fire before wheeling to give way to the next rank. This allowed a continuous fire that could disrupt a static infantry formation. The *Reiters* would then move in, swords drawn, to break it completely.

The Catholic commander felt nervous about this large mass of cavalry. The battlefield was open and sloped toward his line, making it perfect for a charge by the Protestant horsemen. He anchored his line between two villages that would secure his flanks and set his infantry at the front, with the Swiss pike formations taking the center. The Protestants, as expected, moved their cavalry forward as their main form of attack, with the infantry, including the Landsknechts, forming a second line to the rear.

The Protestants started the battle with a mass of cavalry attacking the left of the Catholic line, thus avoiding the Swiss. The line buckled and disintegrated under the massive force of all that heavy cavalry and fled. Much of the cavalry pursued the fleeing infantry, cutting them down and proceeding well to the rear to loot the Catholic baggage train instead of staying to continue the battle. This lack of discipline was common in medieval and Renaissance armies, but enough cavalry remained to put pressure on the Catholic center, where the Swiss pikemen held firm. Repeated attacks inflicted heavy casualties on the Swiss, but they did not give ground. When the Landsknechts moved in, the Swiss made quick work of them and shifted to the left, trying to recapture the Catholic guns that had been overrun in the initial Protestant charge.

Another charge from the Protestant heavy cavalry stopped this. The Swiss, exhausted and their numbers reduced from intense fighting, finally broke. What the Protestant cavalry should have done at this point was to hit the Catholic right, the only part of the line remaining intact, roll it up, and finish their enemy off. Instead, they joined their comrades looting the baggage train. Only the Protestant infantry remained to take the Catholic line.

At this point, the Catholics had a stroke of luck. Reinforcements arrived, and they pushed against the Protestant infantry. The Landsknechts, seeing how the battle was shifting, retreated without a fight, and the rest of the infantry soon followed. The Protestant cavalry, tired and in disorder, saw their backup quitting the field and decided to withdraw as well.

During this chaos, the Prince of Condé was captured, and his second in command, Gaspard de Coligny, made a desperate bid to save the situation. He organized about a thousand French and German cavalry out of the melee and sent them on a charge against the Catholic line. Unfortunately for them, they came up against a crack Catholic unit of arquebusiers and pikemen. The arquebusiers cut them down while the pikemen held them at bay. The French cavalry had used up their lances and had nothing with which to face the pikes. The Germans *Reiters* fired their pistols, but they were insufficient, and finally Gaspard de Coligny called a retreat.

The victory went to the Catholics, but at a heavy cost. They had lost 3,000 infantry and 1,000 cavalry, and their baggage train was thoroughly ransacked. The Protestants had suffered 3,000 casualties, mostly infantry, as well as 1,500 men captured. In fact, the Catholic army was so weakened that it remained inactive for nearly two months while the Protestants secured much of Normandy. This led to a treaty ending the first phase of the conflict, with the Protestants coming out slightly ahead in the negotiations.

The real victors of this battle were the Swiss. Even though their pike square had eventually broke, it had held firm against an incredibly strong onslaught by the heavy cavalry. This helped their somewhat tarnished brand, and Swiss pike squares continued to be used by the Catholics throughout the Wars of Religion. Indeed, they remained in high demand in other nations for the rest of the century.

A woodcut engraving of the battle

After the early 17th century, the pike square began to lose its value thanks to the increased effectiveness of the musket. The flintlock replaced the matchlock and gave a better rate of fire, up to three shots per minute rather than one. Other technological advances gave it better stopping power and accuracy. Men who had once been armed with pikes were increasingly armed with muskets and bayonets, and the old formations of pikes and halberds could stand no chance against them.

Naturally, the Swiss adapted with the times and began to switch to muskets, and the last Swiss unit in a foreign army discarded their pikes around 1700. The Swiss had special units in many European armies, including 12 regiments in French service. These regiments were commanded by Swiss officers, while overall command was by a French general. The men wore red coats rather than the traditional French blue.

The French crown made long-term deals with individual cantons to hire the men, and they proved to be valuable assets. They fought in many of France's wars and were used by Louis XVI during the French Revolution in 1789. They even made up some of the garrison defending the Bastille against the revolutionary mob that stormed it.

Napoleon made use of Swiss regiments in his wars of

conquest, as he did with men of many nationalities, and other nations that had regiments of Swiss mercenaries included the Netherlands, the British Empire, Sicily, and Spain. One Swiss regiment in Spanish service even ended up fighting a Swiss regiment in French service at the Battle of Bailén during Napoleon's invasion of Spain. They wore blue coats rather than the white coats favored by Spanish troops.

The Swiss government eventually banned the practice of hiring out mercenaries in the 1848 constitution, except where a treaty already existed. These treaties were finally all canceled in the new constitution of 1874.

The sole exception is the famous Swiss Guard of Vatican City, which helps defend one of the world's smallest nations. Founded in 1506, it served as part of the armed forces of the Papal States and as the bodyguard of the Pope. Traditionally they fought with halberds, and their distinctive uniforms, still worn today, are said to have been designed by Michelangelo.

An illustration of the conclave of Pius V, with the Swiss Guard guarding the entrance

The Swiss Guard's uniform

The Swiss Guard saw a great deal of active duty during the Renaissance. Their most famous sacrifice came when 189 of them, nearly their entire force at the time, was killed in the Teutonic Cemetery and on the steps of St. Peter's Basilica during the Sack of Rome in 1527. A large number of Protestant soldiers in the army of the Holy Roman Emperor Charles V, mostly Landsknechts, rebelled over unpaid wages and decided to help themselves to the Vatican's wealth. While the Swiss Guard was all but wiped out, their determined stand allowed Pope Clement VII to escape.

Today, the Swiss Guard's numbers are much diminished and comprise only 135 men. Instead of its original role as part of the armed forces of the Papal States, it is now the personal bodyguard of the pope. The unit makes up much of the pomp and ceremony surrounding the head of the Catholic Church, but their fancy dress and outdated halberds mask the fact that they are all well-trained soldiers who also carry modern small arms and no doubt have heavier armaments that they can retrieve at a moment's notice.

Online Resources

Other books about medieval history by Charles River Editors

Other books about the Swiss mercenaries on Amazon

Further Reading

Bennet, Matthew, et al. *Fighting Techniques of the Medieval World AD 500-AD 1500: Equipment, Combat Skills and Tactics.* Staplehurst, Kent, United Kingdom: Spellmount Ltd, 2005.

Bennett, Matthew and Christer Jorgensen, Michael

Pavkovic, Rob S. Rice, Frederick S. Schneid, Chris Scott. *Fighting Techniques of the Early Modern World 1500-1763*. London, United Kingdom: Amber Books Ltd., 2005.

Browning, Oscar. *The Age of the Condottieri.* London, United Kingdom: Methuen & Co., 1895.

Burkhardt, Jacob. *The Civilization of the Renaissance.* New York City, New York: Penguin Books, 1990.

Charles River Editors and Sean McLachlan. *Warfare in the Middle Ages: The History of Medieval Military and Siege Tactics.* Charles River Editors: 2015.

Charles River Editors and Sean McLachlan. *Warfare in the Era of Pike and Shot: The History and Legacy of the Military Strategies that Ushered in Modern Warfare.* Charles River Editors: 2017.

Charles River Editors and Sean McLachlan. *The Landsknechts: The History and Legacy of the German Mercenaries Who Fought for the Holy Roman Empire.* Charles River Editors: 2020.

Charles River Editors and Sean McLachlan. *The Condottieri: The History of Italy's Elite Mercenaries during the Middle Ages and Renaissance.* Charles River Editors: 2020.

Davies, Jonathan. *The Medieval Cannon 1326-1494.* Oxford, United Kingdom: Osprey Publishing, 2019.

DeVries, Kelly. *Medieval Military Technology.* Peterborough, Ontario, Canada: Broadview Press Ltd, 1992.

Hale, J. R. *War and Society in Renaissance Europe 1450–1620.* Stroud, United Kingdom: Sutton Publishing, 1998.

Hall, Bert. *Weapons and Warfare in Renaissance Europe.* London, United Kingdom: The John Hopkins University Press, 2001.

Hogg, O. F. G. *Artillery: Its Origin, Heyday, and Decline.* London, United Kingdom: C. Hurst & Co, 1970.

Machiavelli, Niccolo. *The Florentine History.* London, United Kingdom: Archibald Constable & Co. Ltd., 1906.

McLachlan, Sean. *Medieval Handgonnes: The First Black Powder Infantry Weapons.* Oxford, United Kingdom: Osprey Publishing, 2010.

Mallett, Michael. *Mercenaries and their Masters: Warfare in Renaissance Italy.* London, United Kingdom: The Bodley Head, 1974.

Miller, Artur Maximilian. *The Landsknechts.* Oxford, United Kingdom: Osprey Publishing, 1976.

Miller, Douglas, and Embleton, Gerry. *The Swiss at War 1300–1500.* Oxford, United Kingdom: Osprey Publishing, 1998.

Murphy, David. *Condottiere 1300-1500: Infamous Medieval Mercenaries.* Oxford, United Kingdom: Osprey Publishing, 2007.

Nicolle, David. *Italian Medieval Armies 1300–1500.* Oxford, United Kingdom: Osprey Publishing, 1983.

Nicolle, David. *Medieval Warfare Source Book, vols I & II.* London, United Kingdom: Arms and Armour Press, 1995.

Oman, Charles. *A History of the Art of War in the 16th century*. London, United Kingdom: Methuen & Co., 1937.

Richards, John. *Landsknecht Soldier 1486-1560.* Oxford, United Kingdom: Osprey Publishing, 2002.

Roberts, Keith. *Pike and Shot Tactics 1590-1660.* Oxford, United Kingdom: Osprey Publishing, 2010.

Free Books by Charles River Editors

We have brand new titles available for free most days of the week. To see which of our titles are currently free, click on this link.

Discounted Books by Charles River Editors

We have titles at a discount price of just 99 cents everyday. To see which of our titles are currently 99 cents, click on this link.

Made in the USA
Middletown, DE
12 July 2021

44045587R00053